ISBN: 978-1790421220

SCSC Publication Number: SCSC-153

Permanent URL: http://scsc.uk/scsc-153

Cover photo by Markus Spiske, temporausch.com. Obtained from https://www.pexels.com/.

The Safety Critical Systems Club (SCSC) is the professional network for sharing knowledge about safety-critical systems. It brings together: engineers and specialists from a range of disciplines working on safety-critical systems in a wide variety of industries; academics researching the arena of safety-critical systems; providers of the tools and services that are needed to develop the systems; and the regulators who oversee safety. Through publications, seminars, workshops, tutorials, a web site and, most importantly, at the annual Safety-critical Systems Symposium (SSS), it provides opportunities for these people to network and benefit from each other's experience in working hard at the accidents that don't happen. It focuses on current and emerging practices in safety engineering, software engineering and product and process safety standards.

This document was written by the Safety of Autonomous Systems Working Group (SASWG), which is convened under the auspices of the SCSC. The goal of the SASWG is to produce clear guidance on how autonomous systems and autonomy technologies should be managed in a safety related context, throughout the lifecycle, in a way that is tightly focused on challenges unique to autonomy. The document was formally released at SSS'19, 5-7 February 2019.

Comments on this document are actively encouraged. These can be emailed to:

saswg-comments@scsc.uk

# Safety Assurance Objectives for Autonomous Systems

The Safety of Autonomous Systems Working Group [SASWG]

January 2019

This page is intentionally blank

# Contents

# 1 Introduction

## 1.1 Document Scope and Purpose

This document represents a first step towards establishing and documenting Recognised Good Practice (RGP) for the safety assurance of Autonomous Systems (AS). It has been authored by the Safety of Autonomous Systems Working Group (SASWG), which is convened under the auspices of the Safety Critical Systems Club (SCSC). Consistent with the SASWG's aims[1], the document focuses on novel challenges associated with autonomy technologies.

The SASWG has adopted a structure that uses frameworks at three distinct levels: system; computation; and architecture:

- The system-level framework addresses what the final autonomous entity should do; what effects it should have on its environment. This is the highest level considered; it presents a black-box view.

- The computation-level framework addresses how this is implemented using software and hardware components. This is the lowest level considered; it presents a white-box view.

- The architecture-level framework addresses how computational (and other) components are composed into a system that meets the requirements identified at the system-level. Some approaches to achieving safety will only be intelligible at this level; the inclusion of a monitor function is one such example. It could be described as a grey-box view.

Table 1 includes two examples that illustrate the distinction between system, architecture and computation within the context of this document.

Table 1: Example Systems, Architecture Components and Computations

| Item | Illustration One | Illustration Two |
|---|---|---|
| System | Autonomous Car | Medical Diagnosis System |
| Example Architecture Components | Mapping Data, Sensors, Engine, Brakes | Scanner, Patient Records, Communication Networks |
| Example Computation | Route Planning | Image Classification (Benign / Malignant) |

By design, the chosen frameworks do not include consideration of staff competencies; likewise, issues that are most appropriately addressed at an organisational, or enterprise, level are also excluded. This approach has been adopted in order to focus the SASWG's efforts on topics that are directly related to AS. Consequently, documents produced by the SASWG are intended to be used alongside, or as a supplement to, an existing Safety Management System (SMS).

This document focuses on AS that use Artificial Intelligence (AI) developed using Machine Learning (ML). Although it is possible to envisage AS that do not use these technologies, AI and ML are considered to represent the greatest assurance challenges. As such, systems that use AI and ML have been the focus of the SASWG's efforts.

---

[1] Available from: https://scsc.uk/ga.

SCSC-153 (Jan 2019)

## 1.2  Document Status

The current document represents the first release of objectives by the SASWG. It provides a small set of objectives, focused on the computation-level, that would be expected to be met in any compelling safety argument for AS. Whilst these objectives are considered useful, it should be noted that they have been developed from a theoretical basis and have not been subjected to practical use.

The computation-level was chosen as the focus for this version for two reasons. Firstly, because the SASWG wanted to gain feedback from the wider community on a single framework before developing all three planned frameworks. Secondly, the computation-level is believed to be the easiest to engage with; consequently, its use supports commenting on both the overall framework approach and the individual objectives within that specific framework.

Future versions will contain additional objectives that address issues at the architecture-level and system-level. Consequently, the objectives listed in this document are judged to be *necessary* to support a safety argument for AS but, by themselves, they are not *sufficient*. More specifically, whilst the guidance contained in this document is intended to be beneficial to those working with AS, including designers, manufacturers, operators and regulators, additional considerations will be required to provide a compelling safety argument.

The document has been released in its current form, as a "draft for discussion" to gain feedback from the wider community on both the specific computation-level objectives that have been developed and the approach that is currently being adopted by the SASWG. Feedback can be provided by emailing the address noted on the inner front cover.

## 1.3  Terminology

The SASWG has deliberately avoided defining the term *autonomous*, preferring to work from examples and assuming that, generally speaking, it is easy to identify whether a specific system is autonomous, even though a general definition is difficult to achieve. The desire to avoid protracted and largely uninformative debates about definitions extends across much of the SASWG's work. Nevertheless, it is helpful to provide outline descriptions for some terms used in this document. Specifically:

- A *system* is, typically speaking, an individual vehicle rather than, for example, a swarm of cooperating vehicles or the control logic for vehicle navigation. The same general level applies to autonomous systems that are not vehicle-based: for example, a system to support medical diagnosis may include patient records, a scanner and communication networks, as well as an autonomous decision-making algorithm. A key concept is that the system can, and would generally be expected to, include elements that are developed using traditional approaches, rather than, for example, ML. Many real-world situations are likely to include "systems of systems".

- An *algorithm* implements, possibly indirectly, aspects of a system's behaviour. Generally speaking, an algorithm would be a single implementation developed using an ML technique, for example, a Neural Network (NN), a Support Vector Machine (SVM) or a random forest. A system may include multiple algorithms.

- A *computation* is the physical embodiment of an algorithm. In some contexts, the words are largely interchangeable. A key distinction is that computation includes considerations related to supporting software and to computational hardware; neither of these is included within algorithm.

- A system, or algorithm, is in *operational use* when it is being used for its intended purpose; that is, when its outputs have real-world consequences. Note that it is possible for learning to continue whilst a system, or algorithm, is in operational use.

- A *data set* is used to train, test and verify an algorithm using ML techniques. The part of the data set used to develop the algorithm is referred to as *training data*; the part used for testing is *test data*. Both training data and test data tend to be used by the development team. A separate data set, termed *verification data* may be used for assurance, independent of that team. Note that these definitions apply when the data is used as part of a pre-deployment training and development phase, as well as when there is continual learning.

- The data set is made up of a number of *samples* (e.g., images from a camera). Each sample comprises a number of *features* (e.g., the colour of a given pixel in that scene). The collection of features defines the *input domain*. During operational use the algorithm is provided with *inputs*.

- Providing the algorithm with an input (or, during development, a sample) results in an *output*. This description includes cases where an algorithm uses multiple samples (e.g., streaming data) and cases where the output is multi-dimensional (e.g., a vector of class-membership probabilities).

## 1.4   Document Structure

The remainder of this document is structured as follows:

- Section 2 describes the computation-level framework that has been adopted by the SASWG.

- Section 3 discusses computation-level objectives.

- Section 4, Section 5, Section 6 and Section 7 are included as place holders. The first two of these relate to the architecture-level framework and objectives, respectively. The latter two relate to similar items for the system-level. These sections will be populated in a future version of this document.

- Section 8 contains a summary list of objectives.


- Appendix A provides justification for the computation-level framework.

- Appendix B provides additional justification (beyond that which is included in Section 3) for the computation-level objectives.

- Appendix C contains a list of known issues, which will be resolved in future versions.

- Appendix D contains a list of abbreviations.

- Appendix E contains a list of references.

- Appendix F contains a list of contributors.

This page is intentionally blank

# 2 Computational-Level Framework: Description

This section describes the framework adopted by the SASWG for computation-level considerations. It is a slightly extended version of the one presented by Faria in [16]. The justification for adopting this framework is provided in Appendix A.

The framework consists of six projections, each of which views the computation's properties along a different axis. The projections are not intended to be independent: they are different ways of viewing the same thing. To facilitate discussion, the projections have been arranged in an approximate hierarchical order, working from more abstract to more concrete considerations, specifically: adaptation; experience; task; algorithm; software; hardware. Each of these projections is considered, in turn, in the following sub-sections. The section concludes with a brief tabular summary of the entire framework.

## 2.1 Projections

### 2.1.1 Adaptation

This projection focuses on management and control of changes to the algorithm after its initial operational use. Specifically, it focuses on updates that would not be produced by following the full engineering process associated with development of an algorithm using ML techniques.

It includes, for example, considerations related to on-line learning and provision of nightly updates. In cases where multiple algorithms are deployed operationally (e.g., across a fleet of vehicles, or in multiple data centres), it also includes adaptation at the "population" level (e.g., whether all vehicles, or data centres, are simultaneously updated to the same version of the algorithm, or whether some diversity is deliberately maintained).

### 2.1.2 Experience

This projection focuses on the data set used to train and develop the algorithm. When relevant, this also includes training that continues during operational use, based on the data set provided by the system's experiences.

It includes consideration of how the data was generated, or collected, as well as the use of pre-existing data sets and the nature of any preprocessing activities (e.g., to synthesise missing values). It also encompasses whether the training data is suitably representative of data that is observed (or expected to be observed) during operational use; this includes consideration of the environment(s) associated with the training data. The type of configuration management applied to the data is also relevant within this projection.

### 2.1.3 Task

This projection focuses on the performance of the computation. As such, it is mainly concerned with requirements, that is, what the system requires from the algorithm.

It includes the metrics that are used to measure performance, as well as the performance threshold required to allow the algorithm to be used safely within a system (which may depend on the intended operating environment). Items like accuracy, precision and recall are relevant here although, by themselves, they may not be sufficient. There may, for example, be a need to provide confidence in an algorithm's output. Additionally, there may be a need to demonstrate some non-functional characteristics (e.g., an output will always be provided within a given time).

### 2.1.4  Algorithm

This projection focuses on the choice of algorithm, for example, whether an NN, a SVM, a random forest, or some other approach is used. As such, it is mainly concerned with providing justification for decisions relating to the chosen implementation.

It includes the choice of any hyper-parameters associated with the algorithm: for example, the structure of, and activation function used within, a NN, or the number of trees in a random forest. It also includes decisions related to the training process: for example, the number of training epochs that are used, or the stopping condition that is implemented.

### 2.1.5  Software

This projection focuses on the software instantiation of the algorithm; that is, the translation of mathematics or pseudo-code into a form that can be directly executed on computational hardware. More specifically, this projection is concerned with whether the implementation is a valid representation of the algorithm.

The projection includes the choice of programming language. It also includes the choice of software libraries used to support the development and operational implementation of an algorithm. Tools used to support software development and verification are also captured in this projection.

The choice of, for example, programming language and supporting tools may be different during training than in operational use. Hence, it is convenient to consider this projection twice: once from a training and development perspective and once from the perspective of operational use of the algorithm.

Many of the considerations relevant for this projection are adequately addressed by existing software safety standards.

### 2.1.6  Hardware

This projection focuses on computational hardware. It includes consideration of the type of hardware, for example: Central Processing Unit (CPU); Graphical Processing Unit (GPU); Tensor Processing Unit (TPU); Field Programmable Gate Array (FPGA). It also includes whether this hardware is dedicated to one algorithm or whether it is used to support multiple algorithms (or multiple system features, including non-AI ones).

As with the previous projection, it is convenient to consider the hardware projection from both development and operational use perspectives.

Like the previous projection, many of the considerations relevant for this projection are adequately addressed by existing (computational) hardware safety standards.

## 2.2  Summary

Table 2 provides a brief summary of the six projections in the computation-level framework that has been adopted by the SASWG.

Table 2:  Summary of Projections Within the Computation-Level Framework

| Projection | Outline |
|---|---|
| Adaptation | Focused on how updates to the algorithm are implemented |
| Experience | Focused on the data that is available to train (or develop) the algorithm |
| Task | Focused on the performance of the implemented algorithm; emphasizes requirements |
| Algorithm | Focused on the type of algorithm that is used; emphasizes implementation |
| Software | Focused on the software used to develop the algorithm and, separately, support its operational use |
| Hardware | Focused on the computational hardware that is used, both for development and for operational use |

This page is intentionally blank

# 3 Computational-Level Framework: Objectives

This section lists the objectives associated with each projection of the computation-level framework. Consistent with the SASWG's aims, these objectives focus on autonomy-related challenges; they are not intended to cover all aspects of system development and use.

Each objective is accompanied by a discussion, which illustrates how the objective contributes to the safe use of a computation within an AS. This is followed by examples of approaches that could be taken to satisfy, or partially satisfy, the objective. Note that these examples are not intended to be prescriptive; there may be other ways of satisfying an objective. Likewise, the examples do not necessarily represent a preferred way of satisfying an objective. They are included solely to demonstrate the feasibility of satisfying at least part of the objective.

Currently, this document makes no distinction between different types of computation. Likewise, no distinction is made between computations of different levels of safety criticality; that is, there is no equivalent of Safety Integrity Levels (SILs) or Development Assurance Levels (DALs). These types of distinction may be included in future versions of this document. Currently, users of this document may provide evidence-based, structured arguments to justify why a particular objective need not be considered for their particular computation. Similarly, users may also argue why a particular objective needs only to be covered at a superficial level.

## 3.1 Adaptation

In some cases, an instance of a computation (i.e., the software and hardware that embody an algorithm) may be left unaltered after it is deployed into operational use. Alternatively, all subsequent releases may progress through a full engineering development process. If either of these approaches is adopted then the adaptation projection is not relevant to that computation.

However, it is expected that most computations developed using ML techniques will be adapted in some way following their initial operational use. This could be achieved using a variety of mechanisms, including: online learning (where the algorithm continues learning and, consequently, adapts during operational use); and nightly over-the-air updates (which are released after a reduced amount of regression testing, rather than following the full engineering process).

There are three objectives associated with this projection.

**COM1-1:**     **Inappropriate or unauthorised adaptations should not occur.**

**Discussion:** Fundamentally, an adaptation changes some aspect of the algorithm's behaviour. This means adaptations have the potential to undermine an assurance case and will need to be managed carefully.

For the purposes of this objective, an *inappropriate* adaptation would be one that did not achieve the intended aims. As such, the notion of what is inappropriate is, inevitably, context specific. Potential examples include an adaptation that: unintentionally reduces the algorithm's performance in common situations; unintentionally reduces the algorithm's performance in rare situations; alters the algorithm's non-functional behaviour in a way that detrimentally affects interfacing items. An adaptation that was *incorrect*, perhaps because it did not correspond to the expected information format, would also be considered to be inappropriate.

Conversely, an *unauthorised* adaptation would be one that was made without appropriate authorisation. This could, for example, occur if a malicious third party, or a rogue employee, implemented an adaptation that was intended to cause harm. Alternatively, an adaptation that was released by the algorithm developers but which had not completed the necessary pre-release processes would also be considered unauthorised.

**Examples:** Since it uses a very distinct approach it is simplest to consider online learning as a special case. This is most commonly achieved via Reinforcement Learning (RL). There are a variety of approaches to ensuring adaptations via RL are appropriate, including: constraining the optimisation criterion; adopting a risk-sensitive optimisation criterion; having the algorithm ask for help; and using risk-directed exploration [18]. Alternatively, or additionally, it may be possible to provide a set of abstract policies that formally constrain the exploration of an RL agent [32] or including a representation of fear within the learning mechanism [31].

The nature of online learning is that it happens continuously, as a natural part of the algorithm's use. Hence, the mechanism by which adaptations are achieved forms part of the full engineering cycle associated with initial release to operational use. Consequently, the notion of an unauthorised adaptation does not apply in this case.

For algorithms whose behaviour is not altered by their use, an adaptation involves a deliberate act, typically loading new parameters (or hyper-parameters). For example, in the case of an NN, an adaptation may involve loading new network weights and biases. Considerations associated with Parameter Data Items (PDIs) are important, for example, the data being managed as a distinct entity and its effect on algorithm behaviour being understood [41].

Some form of testing would be expected to be conducted before an adaptation was performed. This should be sufficient to prevent cases where the adaptation unintentionally reduces the algorithm's performance in common situations. One way of achieving this would be to define a collection of situations, along with a minimum level of performance in each. Adaptations would only be considered *appropriate* if at least the minimum level of performance (including safety and security) was achieved in each situation. This collection of situations can be viewed as being analogous to a minimal set of regression tests for traditional software. It can also be viewed as analogous to the criteria used to validate flight simulation training devices [15]. Note, however, that aviation is a well-understood domain. Determining an appropriate collection of situations is likely to be more difficult in many other domains. Also note that the collection may need to change, either in response to changes in the algorithm, or changes in the external environment in which the system is used.

Protecting against the case where the adaptation unintentionally reduces the algorithm's performance in rare situations is more difficult. In many cases a balance has to be found between enacting an adaptation that will demonstrably benefit algorithm performance in common situations against the possibility that the same adaptation could reduce performance (in a way that affects safety) in rare situations. An evidence-based, structured argument is likely to be required to demonstrate that an appropriate balance has been achieved. Although they are out of scope for the current document, it is noted that features of the system architecture (e.g., run-time monitors) could protect against egregious safety failures; if present, these could simplify the "balance" argument.

There are several aspects to understanding how an adaptation may affect interfacing items. Broadly speaking, three categories of interfacing item can be considered: items within the same system as the algorithm; items within other systems; and interactions with humans.

Although it is out of scope of the current document, system-level testing ought to ensure the adaptation does not adversely affect interfacing items within the system. Likewise, system-level testing also ought to cover (planned) interactions with other systems.

Interactions with humans are more subtle, especially if the human requires training or certification in order to use the algorithm. In this case, the impact of the adaptation on user training or certification needs to be considered. These considerations need to take account of not just the latest adaptation, but the cumulative effect of all adaptations that have occurred since the last training or certification.

Preventing unauthorised adaptations is, essentially, a cyber security challenge. Guidance on this topic is available from a number of sources, including cyber security principles for connected and automated vehicles [27] (which can be generalised to cover a wide range of autonomous systems) and the National Cyber Security Centre (NCSC)[2].

**COM1-2:**   **Algorithm behaviour should be appropriate before, during and after an adaptation.**

**Discussion:** This objective recognises a number of things, specifically: adaptations should be performed against a known baseline; an algorithm may be in use when an adaptation request (or command) is received; an adaptation cannot be applied instantaneously; and the process of applying the adaptation may fail.

Any of these factors could undermine an assurance argument. Some, like the finite amount of time taken to apply an adaptation, may only undermine an assurance argument for a relatively small amount of time; others, like the consequences of a failed adaptation, may be persistent.

This objective also recognises that many different types of algorithm behaviour may be appropriate. This is a consequence of requirements being implicitly expressed via the training data, rather than being formally decomposed (in a traceable manner) as is the case for traditional safety-related software.

**Examples:** If all objectives associated with this framework have been satisfied then the algorithm behaviour ought to be appropriate before an adaptation is applied. Hence, that part of the objective is not discussed in detail.

In some cases it may be possible to instantiate two (or more) copies of an algorithm. Such an arrangement would allow one instantiation to adapt whilst the other continues to respond to operational inputs; it would also have the additional benefit of increasing reliability in the context of hardware failures. If two copies are available then the system can determine a suitable time to switch from one (i.e., the pre-adaptation algorithm) to the other (i.e., the post-adaptation model). This switch can be implemented in software, meaning it can be completed without a noticeable impact on the algorithm's ability to respond to operational inputs. More specifically, this arrangement provides a means of demonstrating that algorithm behaviour remains appropriate during an adaptation.

If two (or more) copies are not available then the algorithm is likely to have to stop processing operational inputs before allowing the adaptation to occur. This will require communication between the algorithm and the system to ensure the gap in processing can be accommodated safely. For example, in the case of an autonomous car, an adaptation could be postponed until the car is stationary, the parking brake is on, the engine is turned off and there are no people in the vehicle. An alternative may be to designate safe regions (e.g., the owner's garage, the dealer's service area) and only allow adaptations to occur when the vehicle is in one of these regions. Whatever approach is used, care needs to be taken to protect against the

---

2   https://www.ncsc.gov.uk/.

possibility of vehicles or, more generally, systems not being in a situation where an adaptation is allowed for a prolonged period of time. Additionally, care needs to be taken to prevent removal of the system from the safe region until the adaptation is complete (and confirmed successful).

Some aspects of ensuring that behaviour is appropriate after an adaptation are covered by the *appropriate* part of Objective COM1-1. The current objective is concerned with cases where the adaptation process did not complete successfully. Failed adaptations should be detectable using standard approaches to data integrity and post-adaptation Built-In Test (BIT). In many cases, the most suitable way of handling a failed adaptation is to revert to the previous "last known good" configuration. This requires storing the pre-adaptation algorithm parameters in some way (which happens naturally if there are multiple instantiations of the algorithm).

In some cases (e.g., when the adaptation addresses a serious flaw in the algorithm) reversion to the previous configuration may not be possible, regardless of whether this is readily available. It follows that every system ought to be capable of being put in a safe state that can be maintained for a considerable period.

**COM1-3:**     **There should be an appropriate level of commonality across multiple instantiations of an algorithm.**

**Discussion:** Typically, multiple instantiations of an algorithm would be expected to be in operational use at the same time. This would be the case if, for example, an autonomous vehicle manufacturer had sold multiple vehicles, because each vehicle would contain an instantiation of the algorithm. Indeed, cases where an algorithm is unique, in the sense of there only being one operational instantiation at any given time, might be quite rare.

If multiple instantiations are in operational use then each instantiation would be expected to comply with all objectives. Nevertheless, having multiple instantiations provides an opportunity to enhance fleet-wide safety. Consider, for example, a large multi-national organisation responsible for running many data centres. Every data centre would not be expected to be run at precisely the same software patch level. In this context, diversity in patch levels offers protection against an unknown common mode failure affecting all data centres. In addition, it allows for changes to be tested in a small number of data centres before they are gradually rolled out.

Conceptually, diversity offers the same benefit for algorithms used in autonomous systems. However, in this case, a balance needs to be found between the known risks associated with an older implementation of the algorithm and the potentially unknown risks associated with a newly-produced implementation. An incorrect balance would adversely affect the algorithm's assurance argument.

It should also be noted that fleet-level diversity will naturally arise if the algorithm exhibits online learning. In this case, appropriate measures need to be in place to monitor and control this diversity. Otherwise, two apparently identical autonomous systems may exhibit very different behaviours; this could confuse users (and interacting systems) with potentially unsafe results.

**Examples:** The first step in managing diversity across algorithm instantiations within a fleet is to gain information on the individual algorithms [2]. This could involve reporting from every autonomous system, or from a suitably-sampled subset of them. With this information, the algorithm developer is able to replicate the algorithm's behaviour in a synthetic environment (that has been demonstrated to be suitably representative).

This allows the developer to measure the performance of the algorithm in a number of standard scenarios (or situations). The choice of scenarios would be expected to be described and justified as part of the algorithm's assurance argument. Care needs to be taken to ensure that the selection of scenarios is suitable for the intended use. However, experience from other areas suggests this may be possible: for example, a standard set of situations is used when testing an aircraft flight simulator [15]. The notion of situation coverage could also inform this decision [1].

Using standard scenarios provides a practical measure of the impact of diversity across the various algorithm instantiations. This may be supplemented by a theoretical measure of diversity, which could be calculated by sampling inputs from across the algorithm's input domain and comparing the results provided by different instantiations.

## 3.2 Experience

The experience projection is focused on the training data that is used to develop the algorithm. This data is crucially important because it encodes the requirements that the algorithm has to satisfy. Unfortunately, this encoding is implicit, in the form of the desired input-output relationship, so it cannot be directly examined. Hence, assurance that the algorithm's behaviour will be appropriate has to include aspects relating to the data.

There are four objectives associated with this projection.

**COM2-1**: **The data should be acquired and controlled appropriately.**

**Discussion:** Data is obviously a very important part of an ML approach. Consequently, any assurance argument that addresses the ML-produced algorithm also has to address the data used to support its development. More particularly, if the source of the training, test and verification data cannot be adequately defined, or if this source is not appropriate for the intended use, then it will be difficult to produce a compelling assurance argument.

**Examples:** The first part of this objective relates to the way the data is acquired. For example, this could involve observing an natural process over which little control can be applied, or it could involve controlled trials; alternatively, it could involve the use of a synthetic environment from which training data is generated.

Ideally, the data would be acquired in a controlled manner using a documented process, which takes account of the prevailing environmental features (e.g., weather, system architecture) during collection. Changes to the acquisition method would be formally managed. Also, any software used to support data acquisition would be shown to be correct. In some ways, these considerations mirror those related to the use of Product Service History (PSH) in the aviation domain [8].

If a complete data set is acquired from an external party then care should be taken to ensure that it has not been subject to "Data Poisoning"; for example, the addition of a small number of maliciously crafted samples can create a backdoor [9]. The same techniques used to confirm the authenticity of information downloaded from the Internet (e.g., checksums) may be helpful here. When using data from an external party, care also needs to be taken to ensure it is not accidentally flawed, for example, because of translation issues (e.g, through different use of common terms like "speed").

Regardless of how the data is acquired there is also a need to analyse and quantify uncertainty. This may arise, for example, from sensor noise when measuring samples. Another potential source is labelling uncertainty: for example, should a person walking next to a bicycle be classified as a pedestrian or a cyclist? This can be an issue if labelling is conducted by a team of humans [12].

The second part of this objective relates to control of the data. More specifically, the data would be expected to be subject to some form of configuration management process, which protects it from accidental or unauthorised changes. Standard configuration management tools are likely to be suitable for this purpose, although the large-scale, often static, nature of training data may mean they are not optimal.

Note that algorithms featuring online learning will continue to receive training data during operational use. This indicates there may be a need to include safeguards so that only suitable data is used for learning purposes. These could, for example, check that inputs are sufficiently similar to those that have been seen before, either because they were included in the original, pre-deployment training data or because they have previously been observed in operational use; these two conditions allow gradual expansion of the range of suitable data as the algorithm learns. The notion of "sufficient similarity" bears some relation to the concept of distribution shift[3] [35], but here it involves comparing a single sample with a distribution, rather than the more typical case of comparing two distributions.

**COM2-2:** **Pre-processing methods should not introduce errors.**

**Discussion:** Just because data has been collected in a controlled manner (as indicated by the preceding objective), it does not necessarily follow that the data is suitable for training an algorithm. In many ML applications, there is a step between acquiring data and having data in a form suitable for algorithm development. This step generally involves pre-processing the data. It could include, for example, detecting missing data items and replacing them with suitable surrogate values; it could also include normalising features. Since pre-processing directly affects the data used to develop the algorithm, any errors in pre-processing could undermine a computation-level assurance argument.

Pre-processing is likely to occur during operational use as well. For example, raw sensor readings are likely to be processed in some way before being provided as inputs to an algorithm. Although it is important, this type of pre-processing is considered to be a system-level issue, rather than a computation-level issue. Consequently, it is out of scope for the current discussion.

**Examples:** Typically, pre-processing would be expected to be achieved using traditional types of software. This means that the approaches used to provide assurance for traditional software are also applicable here. In addition, pre-processing software bears some similarities to tools used to support traditional software development. One way of achieving confidence that those tools do not introduce errors is the notion of Tool Qualification. Hence, concepts like Tool Qualification Levels (TQLs) [42] are also relevant. In that specific context, pre-processing software can be considered as a tool that can introduce errors into the operational software (rather than a tool that can only fail to detect an error).

**COM2-3:** **The data should capture the required algorithm behaviour.**

**Discussion:** Even if the data is suitable for training an algorithm, it does not necessarily follow that it is suitable for training a *specific* algorithm. Fundamentally, training data encodes the requirements that the algorithm's behaviour is intended to satisfy, so a data set suitable for training an algorithm to recognise road signs will not be suitable for training an algorithm to recognise human emotions. Unfortunately, the

---

[3]    Distribution shift is also considered in Objective COM2-4

data does not encode the requirements in an explicit manner. Consequently, these requirements cannot be directly reviewed by stakeholders or algorithm developers. This means an argument needs to be made as to why a particular set of data is appropriate for a specific algorithmic behaviour.

**Examples:** Exploratory data analysis [50] would be a sensible first step in understanding the properties of a data set and, consequently, its applicability to a particular algorithm. This could include plotting marginal distributions of each feature and calculating two-way correlation coefficients. It can also be helpful to identify typical and outlier samples (possibly on a class-by-class basis, for classification problems) [3]. The concept of outlier samples can also be extended to include rare situations, the presence (or absence) of which is likely to be informative. The insights gained from this work can inform discussions involving domain experts and ML specialists, as well as supporting an assurance argument.

In essence, part of this objective is about understanding the relationship between the training data and the algorithm's application domain. In some cases, this relationship can be quite subtle. Consider, for example, an algorithm intended to recognise British traffic signs. Despite the restriction of the algorithm's domain to British traffic signs it may be appropriate to train it on British, Continental European, and worldwide, traffic signs. Along with apparent economic benefits (e.g., if the same algorithm could subsequently be employed in different markets), this approach could increase algorithm robustness.

A related, but more extreme, version of this general approach is transfer learning, where a pre-trained network is specialised, or fine-tuned, for a specific task. This approach is often used for image recognition tasks. In this case, the nature of the pre-trained network would be expected to be discussed in any assurance argument. This discussion would also be expected to address the possibility of the pre-trained network introducing a backdoor, or otherwise undesirable, behaviour [21].

**COM2-4**: **Adverse effects arising from distribution shift should be protected against.**

**Discussion:** Distribution shift occurs when the operational inputs provided to the algorithm differ, in a statistically meaningful sense, from the samples used during development. This is important because, in addition to encoding requirements, training data also captures information relating to the domain in which the algorithm can safely be used.

**Examples:** There are a number of different types of distribution shift, including cases where the inputs change and cases where the input-output relationship changes [35]. The possibility of each type of distribution shift would be expected to be considered and appropriate protection provided. Any detection of distribution shift is statistical in nature. This means that a balance needs to be struck between the possibility of false alarms (i.e., false positives) and the probability of false negatives; this balance may be a hard wired feature, or it may be tuneable.

Since the algorithm is meant to generalise the input-output mapping of the training data, there are dangers in taking too rigid a statistical approach. More specifically, the inputs seen by the algorithm during operational use are not expected to be precisely the same as those used during training. Consequently, the algorithm may be better suited to providing operational predictions for inputs that lie inside (i.e., within the convex hull of) the training data than to providing predictions for inputs that lie outside the training data.

There are other reasons why a naive comparison of training and operational distributions is likely to be inappropriate. For example, to increase robustness the training data may be supplemented with adversarial examples [20]. Additionally, the frequency of "rare but important" examples may be artificially increased within the training data by generating synthetic data.

Also note that, in some cases, data can be statistically similar, but semantically different. Consider a distribution with zero mean, that is symmetric about this value; swapping the sign on all samples would produce a data set that was statistically similar, but semantically different. This possibility should be considered and, if appropriate, protected against.

From a computation-level perspective, the focus is on detecting distribution shift. Appropriate responses are best enacted at either the architecture-level or the system-level.

## 3.3   Task

This projection is focused on the performance of the algorithm; that is, whether it can be safely used within the intended system context. As with traditional safety-related software, requirements would be expected to be passed down from the system-level. Whilst there are some similarities, there are also some differences between evidence that traditional software satisfies its requirements and the corresponding evidence for algorithms developed using ML techniques. This evidence is, obviously, an important component of an assurance argument.

There are seven objectives associated with this projection.

**COM3-1**:       **The functional requirements imposed on the algorithm should be defined and satisfied.**

**Discussion:** Ultimately, the algorithm is expected to be used as part of a system. In order to perform as part of that system, the algorithm will have to satisfy a number of functional requirements. For example, rather than returning a single prediction, it could be required to return a probability vector that expresses the likelihood of an input belonging to each of a collection of classes. Alternatively, or additionally, it may be required to provide some measure of confidence in its prediction.

**Examples:** Traditional software testing techniques may be helpful in demonstrating some of an algorithm's functional properties. Depending on the criticality of the algorithm, these may involve formal review of test cases and tests being independently conducted (and witnessed).

In ML approaches, functional requirements are not systematically decomposed into low-level requirements that can be unambiguously coded against. This means that traditional software testing techniques should be supplemented by other types of testing. These could include the types of test that are more traditionally seen at the system-level.

Note that the performance of the algorithm is considered in Objective COM3-3.

**COM3-2**:       **The non-functional requirements imposed on the algorithm should be defined and satisfied.**

**Discussion:** The algorithm will be embodied in a wider system. This means it will have to satisfy some non-functional requirements. For example, it may be required to produce an answer within a given time.

**Examples:** As discussed in Objective COM3-1, traditional software testing techniques may be helpful in demonstrating some of an algorithm's non-functional properties, but they should be supplemented by other forms of testing. This could be informed by a set of standard scenarios [10], or situations (as

SCSC-153   (Jan 2019)

discussed in Objective COM1-3).

This will depend, however, on the technologies in use. AS often use novel technology, and it may be that there are no established techniques for measuring a given non-functional property.

A key non-functional requirement for traditional safety-related software is execution time. Consequently, significant effort is often expended measuring (or, in some cases, calculating) the Worst Case Execution Time (WCET). Many algorithms developed using ML techniques will apply exactly the same computational process, regardless of the input; this is the case for NNs, for example. This means that establishing WCET for these algorithms may be no worse than is the case for traditional software.

There are, however, uses of AI for which this is unlikely to be the case; route planning is a possible example. In such circumstances, WCET estimates would be expected to be guided by both knowledge of the algorithm and the likely ways in which it will be used.

**COM3-3**:    **Algorithm performance should be measured objectively.**

**Discussion:** Fundamentally, this objective is about *how* performance is measured. The question of what level of performance is required is, essentially, a system-level concern.

Typically, an algorithm would be expected to achieve at least a minimum level of performance. For classification algorithms, this often involves measuring properties like precision, recall or accuracy. These are measured using a validation data set, which is withheld from the training process for this purpose. Note, however, that this involves a statistical measure of correctness.

**Examples:** Although they can be useful, there are limits to what can be gained from measuring properties like precision, recall and accuracy. For example, the existence of adversarial inputs (i.e., inputs that are very close to a sample in the training data, but which are confidently predicted as belonging to a different class) for well-performing algorithms (e.g., [49]) indicates these measures are unlikely to capture all relevant features of algorithm behaviour.

Special care needs to be taken if the data set is imbalanced; for example, if in a classification problem a large proportion of the data falls within a single class. In such cases poorly chosen performance measures can be dominated by the algorithm's performance on the large class [23].

**COM3-4**:    **Performance boundaries should be established and complied with.**

**Discussion:** Depending on the nature of the algorithm's input domain, there may be some combinations of features that do not represent a valid input. Consider, for example, the classic Iris data set that is available from the University of California, Irvine (UCI) Machine Learning Repository [13]. This relates information on specific Iris features (e.g., petal sizes) to the associated species of plant. In this case, there is some relationship between the length and width of an Iris petal. Hence, even though it would fall inside an algorithm's input domain, it would be unreasonable to expect the algorithm to predict Iris species for a very wide, very short petal (since this combination does not occur in nature).

More generally, as noted above (in sub-section 3.2), the training, test and verification data encodes information about the region of applicability for the algorithm. Since this data covers the scope over which the algorithm has been developed and tested, this also establishes boundaries (albeit fuzzy ones) within which the measured performance may, in some sense, be expected.

Note that the question of what response should be provided if the algorithm receives an invalid input is best addressed at the system level. As such, it is not considered here. If appropriate, this response could also be extended to realistic, but very unlikely, points in the input domain.

**Examples:** The approach to this objective is similar to that of Objective COM2-4. However, the two objectives differ in that COM2-4 adopts a more theoretical, data-focused approach, whereas this objective takes greater consideration of the wider system and application domain.

**COM3-5:**      **The algorithm should be verified with an appropriate level of coverage.**

**Discussion:** Branch coverage, statement coverage and Modified Condition / Decision Coverage (MC/DC) [11] are well established measures of test coverage for traditional software. These measures, and other related ones, allow judgements to be made regarding the sufficiency of a test set (e.g., one based on the software requirements). More colloquially, in some sense they allow an informed decision to be made that sufficient testing has been achieved.

From the perspective of an algorithm developed using ML approaches there is a similar need to provide objective evidence that a sufficient level of testing has been completed.

**Examples:** Coverage measures would be expected to consider two perspectives: one focused on the input domain; and one focused on the internal features of the algorithm.

Approaches that address the former perspective (i.e., the input domain) are likely to be common across all ML approaches. These may consider the input domain it its raw form (i.e., as measured by system-level sensors); alternatively, they may consider a simpler representation of this data, for example, one developed using Principal Component Analysis (PCA). In some cases, they may also involve approach-specific characteristics, for example, considering the feature space represented by a particular layer in a neural network. However, since this space is dependent on the training data, by themselves these types of consideration would not be sufficient. One option may be to consider characteristic sets that categorise input scenarios (e.g., by weather, road type, traffic level) and then establish a form of combinatorial coverage across these sets [10].

Approaches that address the latter perspective (i.e., algorithm internal features) are likely to be specific to a particular type of algorithm, or family of algorithms. For example, in the case of random forests, a measure of how many branches are covered in each tree by the verification data may be informative. Understanding how this value varies across individual trees in the forest (and, especially, the minimum value) is also likely to be informative. In the case of neural networks, measures based on neuron activations are likely to be helpful [48], especially those based on activations of combinations of (rather than individual) neurons.

Another potentially useful approach to establishing test coverage is that of negation. Consider, for example, a pedestrian detection function. This could be tested with images that: (a) should be classified as containing pedestrians; (b) might be classified as containing pedestrians; (c) should definitely not be classified as containing pedestrians. More generally, the latter class (which can be viewed as negating the requirement) can be an easy way of generating powerful test cases.

**COM3-6:**      **The test environment should be appropriate.**

**Discussion:** Since test results will form part of the assurance argument, there must be confidence in the test environment that produced these results. This environment includes physical assets, software code and test cases. In addition, the test environment would be expected to be under configuration management, so that it could not be arbitrarily changed.

**Examples:** Much of this objective would be satisfied by traditional approaches to the development of safety-critical, or safety-related, software. However, it is possible, perhaps likely, that the test environment will include some representation of the real world, for example, because the test environment includes a representation of the system within which the algorithm is embodied or because it includes a representation of the real world process that generated the training data. In either case, there is a need to validate the representation of the real world entity, or process. This could be achieved using standard approaches for simulation validation [44], potentially supported by a standard set of scenarios (as discussed in Objectives COM1-1 and COM1-3).

Although it is primarily an architecture-level concern, in some cases it may be helpful to include a run-time monitor that compares the representation of the real-world included in the test environment with the world experienced during operational use [17].

**COM3-7:**     **Each algorithm variant should be tested appropriately.**

**Discussion:** For the purposes of this document, it is helpful to distinguish between instantiations, which *may* yield different behaviour (as discussed in Objective COM1-3), and variants, which are *intended* to yield different behaviour. For example, different algorithm instantiations would be expected in all autonomous vehicles operating in the United States of America, whereas different variants would be needed to obey state-level driving laws. More generally, algorithm variants can facilitate adherence to local legislation, or local practices.

**Examples:** The question of how much testing of one variant can be read across into another is, inevitably, situation specific. Nevertheless, the use of algorithm variants has some similarity to the notion of software product line development [37].

## 3.4   Algorithm

Different types of algorithm have different strengths and weaknesses. Hence, the type of algorithm that is used has to be suitable for the task in hand. In particular, the choice of algorithm should be based on the requirements it has to satisfy and the application domain; it should not be an arbitrary choice, nor should it be based solely on developer familiarity.

There are four objectives associated with this projection.

**COM4-1:**     **An appropriate algorithm type should be used.**

**Discussion:** A variety of algorithm types are available, including NNs, random forests, SVMs and RL. There are further divisions within each type. For example, the NN family includes: Deep Neural Networks (DNNs), which feature hidden layers of neurons; Recurrent Neural Networks (RNNs), which have loops within the network structure; and Convolutional Neural Networks (CNNs), which have features designed for image classification.

In most cases, the ML process that produces these algorithms is controlled by hyper-parameters. These may include, for example: the way the available data is split between development and verification activities;

the number of layers, and the number of neurons in each layer, of a NN; the neuron activation function; and dropout rates [47].

**Examples:** Any computation-level assurance argument would be expected to include justification for the chosen algorithm and, also, any hyper-parameters that were used. This could include appropriately-referenced theoretical arguments, for example, arguing that the available literature demonstrates the utility of CNNs in image classification tasks [30].

Empirical arguments are also likely to be required; for example, the performance of a number of different algorithms could be investigated in order to justify the choice of the final algorithm. Likewise, a structured investigation of the effect of different hyper-parameter settings would be expected.

**COM4-2:**     **Typical errors should be identified and shown to be protected against.**

**Discussion:** Broadly speaking, there are four different places where errors can arise: within the training (or verification) data; within the way individual steps are composed to form an algorithm; within a supporting framework; and within the execution environment [55]. These approximately map to the experience, algorithm, software and hardware projections, respectively. Consequently, this objective is concerned with issues relating to ML approaches in general, the class of algorithm and hyper-parameter choices.

**Examples:** Comparatively, there is much less experience as to what typical errors may be in algorithms trained using ML techniques than for traditional safety-related software. Nevertheless, there are some indications of things that should be avoided, including over-fitting, where the algorithm learns the specific data rather than the generic relationship and data leakage, where the algorithm has access to information that should not legitimately be available [24]. Adversarial examples may also be a typical error for large-dimensional data sets [19]. Another typical error may be the under-representation of rare events in the training data [53].

Whilst some indicative typical errors are beginning to emerge, it is less clear how these errors can be detected and corrected. In the specific case of over-fitting, it appears that groups of neurons that fire for a single class may be indicative of memorising the specific training data, rather than generalisation [34].

Although supporting frameworks can simplify the use of ML approaches, their nature can make it difficult to detect errors. For example, many learning processes have stochastic features; this means that bugs are hard to reproduce and, furthermore, success criteria are statistical in nature (which means incorrect code can appear to be working) [55].

**COM4-3:**     **The algorithm's behaviour should be explainable.**

**Discussion:** Algorithms developed using ML approaches do not feature the formal, traceable, hierarchical decomposition of requirements that is typical of traditional safety-related software [4]. This lack of traceable decomposition contributes to a lack of understanding regarding how a specific piece of algorithm behaviour contributes to the final output. Expressed another way, it is easy to see *what* an algorithm is doing; it is less easy to see *why*.

**Examples:** There are two main perspectives that should be considered when thinking about explaining behaviour [22]:

- Explaining a single output from an algorithm. A number of approaches have been proposed, including: training simplified (human-understandable) models to represent the algorithm's behaviour for the input of interest [39]; and providing visual representations [26].

- Explaining algorithm behaviour in general. There is apparently less work in this area. It is notable that behaviour in general cannot be explained by looking at behaviour in even a large number of individual cases: the non-linear nature of many ML-developed algorithms means it is not appropriate to extrapolate from the specific to the general.

The objective of explainable behaviour suggests a preference for low-complexity approaches. However, in isolation, these approaches may not be able to achieve the required level of performance. Combining several algorithms, either in series or in parallel, may be a suitable way forward.

Depending on the way the algorithm is used, the need to explain the algorithm's behaviour, which is an important part of any computation-level assurance argument, may have to be balanced against the possible effects an explanation may have. Consider, for example, a medical diagnosis system that uses doctor's notes as one of many inputs. If the doctors were informed that using a particular word (e.g., "unusual") was a significant trigger for a particular decision from the algorithm, this may change the way they write their notes (which would be a form of distribution shift, so Objective COM2-4 is relevant). Whilst this is a system-level consideration, it is informed by computation-level knowledge.

Although the precise details are outside the scope of this document, it should be noted there may be legal (or ethical) factors that affect the extent to which an algorithm's behaviour has to be explained [51].

**COM4-4**:      **The algorithm should support post-incident analysis.**

**Discussion:** The process of air accident investigation is, arguably, one of the main reasons that air travel is comparatively safe. Given the relative immaturity of autonomous systems, analysis of incidents (including those that do not result in an accident) is likely to make a significant contribution to safety in this field. Consequently, the algorithm is expected to support post-incident analysis.

**Examples:** This objective is related to Objective COM4-3 in that explanation of a single result (or a small number of results) from the algorithm will be an important part of the post-incident analysis. However, sufficient information needs to be recorded to allow the algorithm's behaviour to be reconstructed after the incident. This may involve storing internal state information, including any data used to support non-deterministic choices within the algorithm.

Some aspects of this (e.g., provision of sufficient storage space) are system-level issues. Other aspects may affect both the system and the algorithm: for example, a requirement to support post-incident analysis for anything that has occurred sometime in the last 30 days may drive a different algorithm design to a requirement to support investigations over a 30-second period.

A computation-level assurance argument would be expected to demonstrate that post-incident analysis can be conducted. One way this may be achieved is by treating discoveries during development and testing as pseudo-incidents and confirming that sufficient information was recorded to support post-incident analysis.

## 3.5   Software

Any algorithm will rely on software. Consequently, software needs to be considered in a computation-level assurance argument. The software associated with development of the algorithm is likely to be different to the software employed during operational use. Consequently, it is helpful to consider objectives in the software projection from both development and operational use perspectives.

There are two objectives associated with this projection.

**COM5-1**:         **The software should be developed and maintained using appropriate standards.**

**Discussion:** Even though supporting libraries, or tool kits, are available, at some point an algorithm will almost certainly rely on some traditional-style software (e.g., because this is what the supporting library is implemented in). Faults in this software have the potential to undermine an assurance argument.

**Examples:** Much of this objective is likely to be addressed through the use of an existing standard for safety-critical software development (e.g., [41]). This should help prevent typical errors (e.g., integer overflow) from being introduced. There are, however, a number of areas where an existing standard may not be straightforward to apply.

Firstly, generally speaking, supporting libraries are not developed to such rigorous standards. There are several potential approaches to this challenge. For example, it may be possible to provide additional evidence that relates to the portion of the framework that is actually used. Alternatively, it may be possible to compare the results from different (independently developed) libraries [46]. It may also be possible to re-implement the ML algorithm from scratch (e.g., use a library to investigate multiple algorithms, then re-implement only the chosen one). Whatever approach is adopted, a computation-level assurance argument would be expected to provide a justification as to why any supporting framework is suitable.

Secondly, the pervasive nature of the framework means it is inappropriate to treat it as Software of Uncertain Pedigree (SOUP) [29]. In particular, it is not possible to put the framework in a bounded, protected environment and carefully monitor the inputs and outputs to that environment.

Thirdly, rather than developing an algorithm from scratch, significant savings might be achieved by starting with a pre-trained model. However, there is a possibility that these models could include trapdoors that cause the model to exhibit inappropriate behaviour in very specific circumstances [21]. The nature of these trapdoors means it is unlikely that they will be discovered simply by running tests through the model. Consequently, any use of pre-trained models would be expected to be explicitly justified in any computation-level assurance argument. For example, pre-trained models should be obtained from trusted sources, using a distribution mechanism that provides strong guarantees on integrity.

**COM5-2**:         **Software misbehaviour shall not result in incorrect outputs from the algorithm.**

**Discussion:** Generally speaking, most safety-related systems that use software include protections against software failures or, equivalently, cases where the software does not behave as expected. This prevents errors propagating through the system and allows restorative measures to be implemented (e.g., restarting an application). The key issue is that software misbehaviour is detected and responded to [38].

**Examples:** Algorithms developed using ML approaches do not fail (or misbehave) in the same way as traditional software. In particular, it is not apparent that all failures will be readily detectable from outside the algorithm. Hence, there may be benefit in including some form of BIT in the algorithm, which provides confidence that it is operating as expected [45].

Some algorithms may provide a measure of confidence associated with their output. That is, rather than simply classifying an image as a "cat", the information provided may be a 75% confidence the image is a "cat", a 13% confidence the image is a "dog", and so on. Whilst it may be helpful in some circumstances, this may not be sufficient to fully address this objective, not least because adversarial examples show NN can be confident in their output yet still wrong [49].

## 3.6 Hardware

In order to function, any algorithm will rely on computational hardware. Consequently, hardware needs to be considered in a computation-level assurance argument. The hardware associated with development of the algorithm is likely to be different to the hardware employed during operational use. Consequently, it is helpful to consider objectives in the hardware projection from both development and operational use perspectives.

There are two objectives associated with this projection.

**COM6-1**: **Appropriate computational hardware standards should be employed.**

**Discussion:** Similar to Objective COM5-1, ultimately, any algorithm will run on some form of computational hardware. This hardware needs to be considered in a computation-level assurance argument.

**Examples:** Again, similar to Objective COM5-1, much of this objective may be addressed by existing standards (e.g., [40]). In some cases this may be straightforward; in others, the specialist, complex nature of the hardware may pose challenges. For example, this hardware could include GPUs or TPUs, used for massively parallel calculations; alternatively, it may involve a complex System-on-Chip (SoC), featuring a combination of processor cores, GPUs (or TPUs) and bespoke components (e.g., video coders / decoders).

**COM6-2**: **Hardware misbehaviour shall not result in incorrect outputs from the algorithm.**

**Discussion:** There are several reasons why computational hardware may not behave as expected; Single Event Upsets (SEUs) are one example. Another aspect, specific to algorithms developed using ML techniques, is differences in development hardware and operational hardware (which may mean the operational performance differs from what would be expected).

**Examples:** Any computation-level assurance argument would be expected to consider the possibility of hardware misbehaviour and offer protections against it. This includes SEUs. It also includes the effect of different numerical precisions being used on development and operational hardware, as well as the possibility of non-deterministic behaviour on GPUs, even if the algorithm does not feature non-deterministic components [36].

Considerations relating to Size, Weight and Power (SWaP) may mean the computation hardware used to run the algorithm is also used for other purposes. In such cases, the assurance argument would be expected to demonstrate neither of these uses will interfere with the other. Standard approaches to partitioning are likely to be helpful.

Depending on the system, allocation of software to computational hardware may be fixed at design time or it may be dynamically allocated, possibly changing during operation. In either case, a computation-level assurance argument would be expected to demonstrate that sufficient resources will be available to allow the algorithm to complete its processing within the expected amount of time.

# 4 Architecture-Level Framework: Description

This section will be populated in a later version of the document.

This page is intentionally blank

# 5   Architecture-Level Framework: Objectives

This section will be populated in a later version of the document.

This page is intentionally blank

# 6 System-Level Framework: Description

This section will be populated in a later version of the document.

This page is intentionally blank

# 7  System-Level Framework: Objectives

This section will be populated in a later version of the document.

This page is intentionally blank

# 8 Summary

For ease of reference, this section lists the objectives discussed earlier.

## 8.1 Computation-Level

### 8.1.1 Adaptation

- **COM1-1**: Inappropriate or unauthorised adaptations should not occur.
- **COM1-2**: Algorithm behaviour should be appropriate before, during and after an adaptation.
- **COM1-3**: There should be an appropriate level of commonality across multiple instantiations of an algorithm.

### 8.1.2 Experience

- **COM2-1**: The data should be acquired and controlled appropriately.
- **COM2-2**: Pre-processing methods should not introduce errors.
- **COM2-3**: The data should capture the required algorithm behaviour.
- **COM2-4**: Adverse effects arising from distribution shift should be protected against.

### 8.1.3 Task

- **COM3-1**: The functional requirements imposed on the algorithm should be defined and satisfied.
- **COM3-2**: The non-functional requirements imposed on the algorithm should be defined and satisfied.
- **COM3-3**: Algorithm performance should be measured objectively.
- **COM3-4**: Performance boundaries should be established and complied with.
- **COM3-5**: The algorithm should be verified with an appropriate level of coverage.
- **COM3-6**: The test environment should be appropriate.
- **COM3-7**: Each algorithm variant should be tested appropriately.

### 8.1.4  Algorithm

- **COM4-1**: An appropriate algorithm type should be used.
- **COM4-2**: Typical errors should be identified and shown to be protected against.
- **COM4-3**: The algorithm's behaviour should be explainable.
- **COM4-4**: The algorithm should support post-incident analysis.

### 8.1.5  Software

- **COM5-1**: The software should be developed and maintained using appropriate standards.
- **COM5-2**: Software misbehaviour shall not result in incorrect outputs from the algorithm.

### 8.1.6  Hardware

- **COM6-1**: Appropriate computational hardware standards should be employed.
- **COM6-2**: Hardware misbehaviour shall not result in incorrect outputs from the algorithm.

## 8.2   Architecture-Level

This sub-section will be populated in a later version of the document.

## 8.3   System-Level

This sub-section will be populated in a later version of the document.

# Appendix A  Computation-Level Framework: Justification

This appendix summarises the process used to develop the computation-level framework adopted by the SASWG. In doing so, it provides some justification for the choice of framework. It also provides some confidence that the framework covers all relevant topic areas.

Initially, a small-scale survey of existing computation-level frameworks was conducted. This identified the items listed in Table 3.

Table 3: Computation-Level Frameworks Considered

| Section | Framework |
|---------|-----------|
| A.1.1 | Modified Software Safety Assurance Principles |
| A.1.2 | Slightly Extended "Faria Stack" |
| A.1.3 | Douthwaite and Kelly's "Viewpoints" |
| A.1.4 | Google's Machine Learning Rubric |
| A.1.5 | Ethical and Safety Principles |
| A.1.6 | Burton's "Making the Case" Argument |

Each computation-level framework is briefly summarised (sub-section A.1) and a preferred framework is selected. A top-level mapping between frameworks is completed, to confirm that the chosen framework incorporates all relevant parts of the other computation-level frameworks (sub-section A.2). Similar, top-level mappings from the chosen framework to, firstly, a typical software development approach and, secondly, a generic approach to ML-based development are conducted; these demonstrate the framework provides appropriate coverage of typical development activities (sub-section A.3).

## A.1  Computation-Level Frameworks

### A.1.1  Modified Software Safety Assurance Principles

The first computation-level framework is described in a paper presented at the 2017 SSS [4]. The paper considers the "four plus one" software safety assurance principles [25] from the perspective of non-traditional (e.g., ML / AI) software. A slightly revised and extended set of six (or "four plus two") principles are proposed:

- Principle One: Software safety requirements shall be defined to address the software contribution to system hazards;

- Principle Two-Primed: The software detailed design shall embody the intent of the software safety requirements;

- Principle Three: Software safety requirements shall be satisfied;

- Principle Four: Hazardous behaviour of the software shall be identified and mitigated;

- Principle Four plus One: The confidence established in addressing the software safety principles shall be commensurate to the contribution of the software to system risk;

- Principle Four plus Two: Software required to produce behaviour not predictable at design time should consider the consequence of behavioural adaptations on its environment.

## A.1.2   Slightly Extended "Faria Stack"

The second computation-level framework is a slightly extended version of information presented in a paper at the International Symposium on Software Reliability Engineering (ISSRE) Workshop on Software Certification (WoSoCer) [16]. This framework comprises six projections:

- Adaptation, which considers how the computation is updated (e.g., through online learning, through overnight updates, etc.);

- Experience, which is focused on the data that is available to train a machine learning algorithm;

- Task, which is concerned with the performance of the implemented computation;

- Algorithm, which considers the type of algorithm (e.g., neural network, random forest, etc.);

- Software, which includes considerations such as the language in which the computation is implemented;

- Hardware, which relates to the computational hardware that is used.

When using this framework it may be helpful to consider, at least, the Software and Hardware projections from two perspectives, specifically training and operational use.   For example, it is likely that the computational hardware used for training will be different to that used during an operational deployment.

## A.1.3   Douthwaite and Kelly's "Viewpoints"

The third computation-level framework was presented at the 2018 SSS [14]. Building on the concept of distinct viewpoints used in systems engineering, this paper identifies six viewpoints. Although they were developed from the perspective of Bayesian Networks, the paper suggests the viewpoints are applicable to many types of artificial intelligence software. The viewpoints are:

- Model, which relates to the structure and parametrisation of the model underlying the learnt algorithm;

- Data, which covers all data acquisition, processing and storage concerns (including knowledge engineering and expert elicitation);

- Computational, which includes the properties of all algorithms used for learning and reasoning tasks within the system, their selection process, and the associated assumptions and design decisions;

- Operational, which focuses on the evolution and maintenance of the system after deployment;

- Technology, which covers the necessity, properties, constraints and assumptions of modelling frameworks used in the system;

- Implementation, which addresses all "conventional" software and hardware engineering concerns, including "normal" function allocation, requirements and associated verification and validation activities.

As with the extended "Faria Stack" considered above, there may be advantages in considering some of the above viewpoints from both training and operational perspectives.

## A.1.4  Google's Machine Learning Rubric

The fourth computation-level framework [6] includes a scoring mechanism that is intended to measure how suitable a machine learning approach is for deployment. It is based on computations used in a web-like environment, but may be of relevance to wider autonomous systems.

The framework includes four categories, each of which includes several considerations:

- Tests for Features and Data:

    - Test that the distributions of each feature match your expectations;

    - Test the relationship between each feature and the target, and the pairwise correlations between individual signals;

    - Test the cost of each feature;

    - Test that a model does not contain any features that have been manually determined as unsuitable for use;

    - Test that your system maintains privacy controls across its entire data pipeline;

    - Test the calendar time needed to develop and add a new feature to the production model;

    - Test all code that creates input features, both in training and serving.

- Tests for Model Development:

    - Test that every model specification undergoes a code review and is checked in to a repository;

    - Test the relationship between offline proxy metrics and the actual impact metrics;

    - Test the impact of each tunable hyper-parameter;

    - Test the effect of model staleness;

    - Test against a simpler model as a baseline;

    - Test model quality on important data slices;

    - Test the model for implicit bias.

- Tests for ML Infrastructure:

    - Test the reproducibility of training;

    - Unit test model specification code;

    - Integration test the full ML pipeline;

    - Test model quality before attempting to serve it;

    - Test that a single example or training batch can be sent to the model, and changes to internal state can be observed from training through to prediction;

    - Test models via a canary process before they enter production serving environments;

    - Test how quickly and safely a model can be rolled back to a previous serving version.

- Monitoring Tests for ML:

    - Test for upstream instability in features, both in training and serving;

– Test that data invariants hold in training and serving inputs;

– Test that your training and serving features compute the same values;

– Test for model staleness;

– Test for Not a Number (NaN) or infinities appearing in your model during training or serving;

– Test for dramatic or slow-leak regressions in training speed, serving latency, throughput, or Random Access Memory (RAM) usage;

– Test for regressions in prediction quality on served data.

For each item above, one point is awarded for manual tests (including documenting and distributing the results). A second point is awarded if tests are run automatically and repeatedly. A score is calculated for each of the four categories by adding the scores for each of the listed items. The overall score is then the minimum of these four category scores.

## A.1.5   Ethical and Safety Principles

The fifth framework identifies a perspective on the ethics governing decisions around safety-critical autonomous systems [33]. It aligns with the Modified Software Safety Assurance Principles (discussed above) and is applicable to ethics only so far as these affect safety.

- Principle One: Ethics requirements governing the autonomous system behaviour shall be defined.

- Principle Two: The intent of the ethics requirements shall be maintained throughout decomposition.

- Principle Three: Ethics requirements shall be satisfied.

- Principle Four: Any autonomous system behaviours which conflict with the ethics requirements ("ethically hazardous" behaviours) shall be identified and mitigated.

- Principle Four plus One: The degree of rigour required to address these ethical principles shall be commensurate with the contribution of the autonomous system to system risk.

## A.1.6   Burton's "Making the Case" Argument

The sixth, and final, computation-level framework comes from a paper presented at the 2017 International Conference on Computer Safety, Reliability, and Security [7]. The paper outlines an assurance case structure for a highly automated driving system, which could possibly be extended to cover a wide range of autonomous systems. A Goal Structuring Notation (GSN) approach is used; key features include:

- GOAL G1: The residual risk associated with functional insufficiencies in the object detection function is acceptable;

- CONTEXT C1: Definition of functional and performance requirements on the object detection function;

- ASSUMPTION A1: Assumptions on the operational profile of the system's environment;

- ASSUMPTION A2: Assumptions on attributes of inputs to the machine learning function;

- ASSUMPTION A3: Assumptions on the performance potential of machine learning;

- STRATEGY S1: Argument over causes of functional insufficiencies in machine learning;

- SUBGOAL G2: The operating context is well defined and reflected in training data;

- SUBGOAL G3: The function is robust against distributional shift in the environment;

- SUBGOAL G4: The function exhibits a uniform behaviour over critical classes of situations;

- SUBGOAL G5: The function is robust against differences between its training and execution platforms;

- SUBGOAL G6: The function is robust against changes in its system context.

## A.2   Framework Mappings

Following discussions[4], the SASWG selected the extended "Faria Stack" as the basis for the computation-level framework. The following paragraphs briefly discuss each projection of the extended "Faria Stack", taking into account the other frameworks outlined in the preceding sub-section. Within these discussions:

- For reasons of brevity, only the top-level of Google's Machine Learning Rubric is considered.

- Due to their similarity to the Modified Software Safety Assurance Principles, the Ethical and Safety principles are not explicitly considered.

- For simplicity, only the goals and subgoals are considered from Burton's "Making the Case" Argument.

The discussions also include a "Not Addressed" pseudo-projection, which captures considerations that do not readily relate to any of the projections. By checking the contents of this pseudo-projection, and confirming that it contains nothing significant, confidence can be gained that the adopted framework covers all relevant topics.

### A.2.1   Adaptation

The notion of adaptation is directly related to Principle Four plus Two of the Modified Software Safety Assurance Principles. It is also directly related to Douthwaite and Kelly's Operational viewpoint.

Possible changes between training and operational data relate to the Monitoring Tests for ML category from Google's Machine Learning Rubric, and also to Subgoal G3 from Burton's "Making the Case" Argument.

Using adaptation, or making a conscious decision not to use it, is related to robustness to context changes, which is Subgoal G6 from Burton's "Making the Case" Argument.

### A.2.2   Experience

Consideration of the data used to develop the algorithm directly relates to Douthwaite and Kelly's Data viewpoint, and also to the Tests for Features and Data category from Google's Machine Learning Rubric.

The way the data reflects the operating context directly relates to Subgoal G2 from Burton's "Making the Case" Argument.

---

[4]   SASWG 7, 17 April, York.

### A.2.3   Task

Understanding the task should also include understanding the way it contributes to the wider system and, also, any associated computation (or software) safety requirements. This consideration relates to Principle One of the Modified Software Safety Assurance Principles.

Performance measurement against the intended task ought to include explicit measures against requirements (including safety requirements). It also ought to consider whether the computation has introduced any new hazards. These considerations relate to Principles Three and Four of the Modified Software Safety Assurance Principles. They also relate to Goal G1 from Burton's "Making the Case" Argument.

More generally, performance management relates to the Tests for Model Development category from Google's Machine Learning Rubric.

The properties of the operationally-fielded computation relate to Douthwaite and Kelly's Computational viewpoint.

### A.2.4   Algorithm

The link between choice of algorithm and intended task mirrors the link between requirements (including safety requirements) and detailed design. This relates to Principle Two-Primed of the Modified Software Safety Assurance Principles.

Part of choosing a specific algorithm also includes choosing hyper-parameters (e.g., number of nodes and layers in a neural network). This relates to Douthwaite and Kelly's Model viewpoint. More general algorithm-related choices relate to Douthwaite and Kelly's Computational viewpoint.

### A.2.5   Software

The choice of software (for both development and operational use) is part of detailed design. This relates to Principle Two-Primed of the Modified Software Safety Assurance Principles. It also relates to Douthwaite and Kelly's Technology and Implementation viewpoints, and also to the Tests for ML Infrastructure category from Google's Machine Learning Rubric.

### A.2.6   Hardware

The choice of hardware (for both development and operational use) is part of detailed design. This relates to Principle Two-Primed of the Modified Software Safety Assurance Principles, to Douthwaite and Kelly's Implementation viewpoint, and also to the Tests for ML Infrastructure category from Google's Machine Learning Rubric.

The possibility of different behaviour on development (training) and operational (execution) platforms relates to Subgoal G5 from Burton's "Making the Case" Argument.

## A.2.7 Not Addressed

The chosen computation-level framework does not readily address Principle Four plus One of the Modified Software Safety Assurance Principles: "The confidence established in addressing the software safety principles shall be commensurate to the contribution of the software to system risk". This is not a significant concern as this principle is a cross-cutting issue for all assurance, and thus not something that has to be specifically addressed at the computation level.

In addition, the framework does not readily address Subgoal G4 of Burton's "Making the Case" Argument, "The function exhibits a uniform behaviour over critical classes of situations". It is not immediately clear whether this, especially the "uniform behaviour" part, is a generic requirement that should be satisfied by *every* computation. If it is a requirement for a particular application then it should be addressed by the Task level (via the relationship to Principle One of the Modified Software Safety Assurance Principles).

## A.2.8 Relationship Summary

For ease of reference, the relationships outlined above are summarised in Table 4. Note that this presentation is deliberately simple and top-level.

Table 4: Relationships between Computation-Level Frameworks Considered

| Stack Level | Modified Software Safety Assurance Principles | Douthwaite and Kelly's "Viewpoints" | Google's Machine Learning Rubric | Burton's "Making the Case" Argument |
|---|---|---|---|---|
| Adaptation | Principle Four plus Two | Operational | Monitoring Tests for ML | Subgoals G3 and G6 |
| Experience | - | Data | Tests for Features and Data | Subgoal G2 |
| Task | Principles One, Three and Four | Computational | Tests for Model Development | Goal G1 |
| Algorithm | Principle Two-Primed | Model and Computational | - | - |
| Software | Principle Two-Primed | Technology and Implementation | Tests for ML Infrastructure | - |
| Hardware | Principle Two-Primed | Implementation | Tests for ML Infrastructure | Subgoal G5 |
| *Not Addressed* | *Principle Four plus One* | *-* | *-* | *Subgoal G4* |

## A.3 Software and ML Development Mappings

Table 5 maps the framework's projections to the activities involved in a generic software development [54].

This mapping shows that the chosen computation-level framework is sufficiently complete to address typical software development activities.

Table 5: Mapping Projections to Typical Software Development

|  | Adaptation | Experience | Task | Algorithm | Software | Hardware |
|---|---|---|---|---|---|---|
| Plan | | | Y | | | |
| Requirements | | | Y | | | |
| Design | | Y | Y | Y | | |
| Implement | | Y | Y | Y | Y | Y |
| Test | | | Y | | | |
| Transition | Y | | | | Y | Y |

To provide further confidence, Table 6 maps the projects to the steps that are required to produce a useful ML-based computation [52]. This mapping demonstrates the framework fits well with development in an ML context, with most development steps mapping to a single projection. Note that, since the mapping is to a *development* approach, no mappings to the adaptation projection would be expected (since that projection is concerned with post-development updates).

Table 6: Mapping Projections to Typical ML Development

|  | Adaptation | Experience | Task | Algorithm | Software | Hardware |
|---|---|---|---|---|---|---|
| Frame the question | | | Y | | | |
| Collect data | | Y | | | | |
| Select features | | Y | | | | |
| Choose algorithm | | | | Y | | |
| Choose metrics | | | Y | | | |
| Conduct experiment | | | | | Y | Y |
| Interpret results | | | Y | | | |

# Appendix B   Computation-Level Objectives: Justification

This appendix provides some additional justification for the computation-level objectives listed in the main body. This is achieved by mapping those objectives to separately published material, specifically:

- A suggested list of requirements for a standard to support the use of NNs in safety-critical applications [5]. This source dates from 1996. Consequently, it provides a sound theoretical basis, independent from recent trends, against which computation-level objectives can be compared. However, its considerations do not encompass the latest research directions. In addition, whilst many of its requirements are applicable to a number of ML approaches, they have been derived in the specific context of NNs.

- An analysis of gaps in a current automotive standard with regards to the use of ML approaches [43]. This source dates from 2018, so it encapsulates recent research. However, the chosen standard, specifically International Organization for Standardization (ISO) 26262 [28] is a functional safety standard; that is, it only addresses unsafe behaviours caused by system malfunctions. For ML approaches, there is also a need to consider the Safety Of The Intended Function (SOTIF).

For the reasons outlined above, the computation-level objectives derived by the SASWG would not be expected to directly match the contents of either reference. Nevertheless, the objectives would be expected to cover all relevant issues raised in the reference material.

It is emphasised that the mappings established below are top-level and approximate. This is considered appropriate as the mappings are intended to justify (or, if necessary, refine) the computation-level objectives. More specifically, the mappings discussed in this appendix were not a key part of the process by which the computation-level objectives were derived.

## B.1   Requirements for a NN Standard

Table 7 lists the requirements noted in [5]. Note that these requirements use the term Artificial Neural Network (ANN), rather than NN, which is preferred in the current document. Where appropriate, relevant computation-level objectives are highlighted. If no objectives are relevant, justification for this is provided.

Table 7: Computation-Level Objectives Compared against Requirements for a NN Standard

| Standard Requirement | Relevant Objectives |
|---|---|
| Specify how the high-level goals of, or requirements for, the ANN module are to be obtained | COM3-1, COM3-2 |
| Specify what should be done to ensure that the training data adequately represent the attainment of the high-level goals | COM2-3 |
| Specify what type of networks can be used, and how each type is to be unambiguously designated | COM4-1 |
| Specify how the input-output characteristics are to be unambiguously designated | COM2-1, COM2-2 |
| Specify how the developer must describe the way in which the performance function for the network operates during training | COM3-3 |

| Standard Requirement | Relevant Objectives |
|---|---|
| Specify what details the ANN developer must provide regarding the way in which the ANN module interfaces with the rest of the system | *Out of scope: Architecture-Level* |
| Specify the extent of knowledge, relating to neural networks, required of management and development team personnel | *Out of scope: Staffing* |
| Specify what development model is to be used for the ANN module | COM5-1 |
| Specify any outputs which the ANN module is required to produce in addition to its primary functional output | COM3-1 |
| Specify whether formal methods or rigorous argument are to be used to develop the software which implements the neural network | COM5-2 |
| Specify what methods are to be used for quality assurance in the trained network | COM2-1, COM5-1, COM6-1 |
| Specify that the Verification and Validation (V&V) team should use generalisation tests on the trained network to verify that it has learned the principles implicit in the training data | COM3-3, COM3-6, COM3-7 |
| Specify that the V&V team should validate a Safety-Critical Artificial Neural Network (SCANN) by investigating the behaviour of the SCANN over the whole of the input space | COM3-5 |
| Specify how the developers should check that the initial safety assessments made for the system are not affected by the ANN module and how failures in other modules would affect the system, given the intended operation of the ANN | *Out of scope: System-level* |
| Specify that developers establish possible failure modes of the ANN module itself and the consequences | *Out of scope: System-level (supported by COM2-4, COM3-4, COM4-2, COM5-2, COM6-2)* |
| Specify how Hazard and Operability Study (HAZOP) is to proceed, regarding the operation of network | *Out of scope: System-level* |
| Specify the brief and form of the HAZOP committee, as well as guide words for their use | *Out of scope: System-level* |
| Specify that a certification standard should insist that the developers build the network is such a way that the necessary data are available so that it is possible to do Failure Mode and Effects Analysis (FMEA) and HAZOP | COM4-3, COM4-4 |

It is apparent that all relevant requirements established by [5] are covered by one or more of the computational objectives derived by the SASWG. It is also interesting to note that, firstly, none of the objectives associated with the adaptation projection are included in Table 7 and, secondly, all other objectives are included at least once. The first observation is believed to be a consequence of the age of the reference document; the second provides further confidence that the identified computation-level objectives are necessary.

## B.2   ML-Related Gaps in an Automotive Standard

The analysis of ISO 26262 identified a number of impacted or new Process Requirements (PRs). The associated phase and description are reproduced (from [43]) in Table 8. Relevant computation-level objectives are then highlighted; if there are no such objectives then justification is provided.

Table 8: Computation-Level Objectives Compared against Impacted or New PRs

| Phase | Description | Relevant Objectives |
|---|---|---|
| (5) Initiation | Best practices: coding guidelines | COM4-2, COM5-1 |
| (5) Initiation | ML decision gate | *Out of scope: Architecture-Level* |
| (6) Software safety requirements | Requirements specification | COM2-3, COM3-1, COM3-2 |
| (6) Software safety requirements | Requirements verification | COM3-3, COM3-5 |
| (7) Architectural design | Fault tolerance | *Out of scope: Architecture-Level* |
| (8) Software unit design, implementation | Best practices: notations | COM4-2, COM5-1 |
| (8) Software unit design, implementation | Best practices: design principles | COM4-2 |
| (8) Software unit design, implementation | Best practices: data set collection and verification | COM2-1, COM2-2 |
| (8) Software unit design, implementation | Best practices: model selection | COM4-1 |
| (8) Software unit design, implementation | Best practices: feature selection | COM2-3 |
| (8) Software unit design, implementation | Best practices: training | COM4-2, COM5-1, COM6-1 |
| (8) Software unit design, implementation | Best practices: data set splitting | *Out of scope: Approach-specific* |
| (8) Software unit design, implementation | Best practices: validation | COM3-3, COM4-2 |
| (8) Software unit design, implementation | Best practices: testing | COM3-3, COM3-7, COM5-2, COM6-2 |
| (8) Software unit design, implementation | Best practices: testing structural coverage | COM3-5 |
| (8) Software unit design, implementation | Best practices: test vs. operating environment | COM2-4, COM3-6, COM6-1 |
| (8) Software unit design, implementation | Best practices: test result explanation | COM4-3, COM4-4 |
| (8) Software unit design, implementation | Best practices: verification | COM3-3, COM3-4, COM3-5, COM3-6, COM4-4 |

It is apparent that all impacted or new PRs established by [43] are covered by one or more of the computational objectives derived by the SASWG. It is also interesting to note that, as for the previous sub-section, none of the adaptation-related objectives are used and all other objectives are used at least once. The apparent lack of consideration of the adaptation project may be due to the nature of the source automotive standard, which is focused on a single product release (which may be expected to have much longer time scales than those envisaged under adaptation).

This page is intentionally blank

# Appendix C   Known Issues

This section provides a list of known issues. These are items that were identified, but not resolved, during the creation of the current version of the document. For some issues, resolution is best considered at the architecture-level or the system-level, neither of which is addressed in any detail in the current document. For other issues, resolution needs a greater amount of knowledge and experience than is currently available. In all cases, the issue was deemed sufficiently important to warrant specific capture and tracking.

Note that the following list is not intended to be complete.

- The most obvious known issue relates to analysing the architecture-level and the system-level to derive an appropriate collection of objectives at each level. To help identify and organise these objectives, frameworks will be used at each level.

- At the moment, the document makes no distinction between different criticality levels, for example, DALs or SILs. As exemplified by the last of the "four plus one" software safety assurance principles [25], it is beneficial to target effort towards more critical system elements. In order to achieve this, some form of graduation is necessary. This could be achieved by requiring certain objectives only to be completed at higher criticality levels. Alternatively, higher criticality levels may require some objectives to be completed with independence. Another approach involves addressing an objective more thoroughly as the criticality level increases. It is unclear which combination of these options will be most appropriate for the SASWG's work but, at the current time, it is considered likely that most objectives will need to be satisfied, regardless of criticality level.

- At the moment, the document makes little distinction between different types of ML approach. In some cases this may be captured in the detailed response to an associated with an objective: for example, Objective COM4-2 (discussed in sub-section 3.4) relates to protecting against typical errors, which will differ between different types of ML approach. However, there are several places where a more nuanced approach may be more valuable. One such area is the relationship between the adaptation projection (discussed in sub-section 3.1) and ML approaches that continue to learn during operational use.

- Objective COM3-7 (discussed in sub-section 3.3) notes the difference between algorithm instances, which may produce different results, and algorithm variants, which are expected to produce different results in some circumstances. It is not clear at which point an algorithm ceases to be a variant and becomes something that should be considered as an item in its own right. A key consideration is how easily safety assurance evidence can be transferred between items. More generally, this topic is related to reuse and software product line engineering.

- Currently, the document does not provide much information on integration of Software (SW) and Hardware (HW); neither SW-SW integration nor SW-HW integration is considered in any detail. This collection of issues is expected to extend into the architecture level. As such, it is likely to be addressed in more detail in future editions.

- One particular SW-SW integration issue is the use of multiple algorithms, combined with a voting, or aggregation, function. This represents a potentially useful approach for engineering AS. It is expected that this will be considered as part of the architecture-level.

This page is intentionally blank

# Appendix D   Abbreviations

| | |
|---|---|
| AI | Artificial Intelligence |
| ANN | Artificial Neural Network |
| AS | Autonomous Systems |
| BIT | Built-In Test |
| CNN | Convolutional Neural Network |
| CPU | Central Processing Unit |
| DAL | Development Assurance Level |
| DNN | Deep Neural Network |
| FMEA | Failure Mode and Effects Analysis |
| FPGA | Field Programmable Gate Array |
| GPU | Graphical Processing Unit |
| GSN | Goal Structuring Notation |
| HAZOP | Hazard and Operability Study |
| HW | Hardware |
| ISO | International Organization for Standardization |
| ISSRE | International Symposium on Software Reliability Engineering |
| MC/DC | Modified Condition / Decision Coverage |
| ML | Machine Learning |
| NaN | Not a Number |
| NCSC | National Cyber Security Centre |
| NN | Neural Network |
| PCA | Principal Component Analysis |
| PDI | Parameter Data Item |
| PR | Process Requirement |
| PSH | Product Service History |
| RAM | Random Access Memory |
| RGP | Recognised Good Practice |
| RL | Reinforcement Learning |
| RNN | Recurrent Neural Network |
| SASWG | Safety of Autonomous Systems Working Group |
| SCANN | Safety-Critical Artificial Neural Network |
| SCSC | Safety Critical Systems Club |
| SEU | Single Event Upset |

| | |
|---|---|
| SIL | Safety Integrity Level |
| SMS | Safety Management System |
| SoC | System-on-Chip |
| SOTIF | Safety Of The Intended Function |
| SOUP | Software of Uncertain Pedigree |
| SSS | Safety-critical Systems Symposium |
| SVM | Support Vector Machine |
| SW | Software |
| SWaP | Size, Weight and Power |
| TPU | Tensor Processing Unit |
| TQL | Tool Qualification Level |
| UCI | University of California, Irvine |
| V&V | Verification and Validation |
| WCET | Worst Case Execution Time |
| WoSoCer | Workshop on Software Certification |

# Appendix E   References

[1] R. ALEXANDER, H. R. HAWKINS, AND A. J. RAE, *Situation coverage–a coverage criterion for testing autonomous robots*, University of York, (2015).

[2] R. ASHMORE, *Rethinking diversity in the context of autonomous systems*, in SSS'19 Proceedings, Safety-Citical Systems Club, 2019. To Be Published.

[3] R. ASHMORE AND M. HILL, *Boxing clever: Practical techniques for gaining insights into training data and monitoring distribution shift*, in First International Workshop on Artificial Intelligence Safety Engineering, 2018.

[4] R. ASHMORE AND E. LENNON, *Progress towards the assurance of non-traditional software*, in Developments in System Safety Engineering, Proceedings of the Twenty-fifth Safety-Critical Systems Symposium, Safety-Citical Systems Club, 2017. ISBN 978-1540796288.

[5] D. BEDFORD, G. MORGAN, AND J. AUSTIN, *Requirements for a standard certifying the use of artificial neural networks in safety critical applications*, in Proceedings of the international conference on artificial neural networks, 1996.

[6] E. BRECK, S. CAI, E. NIELSEN, M. SALIB, AND D. SCULLEY, *What's your ml test score? a rubric for ml production systems*, in NIPS Workshop on Reliable Machine Learning in the Wild, 2016.

[7] S. BURTON, L. GAUERHOF, AND C. HEINZEMANN, *Making the case for safety of machine learning in highly automated driving*, in International Conference on Computer Safety, Reliability, and Security, Springer, 2017, pp. 5–16.

[8] CERTIFICATION AUTHORITIES SOFTWARE TEAM, *Guidance for assessing the software aspects of product service history of airborne systems and equipment*, Tech. Rep. CAST-1, Federal Aviation Authority, June 1998.

[9] X. CHEN, C. LIU, B. LI, K. LU, AND D. SONG, *Targeted backdoor attacks on deep learning systems using data poisoning*, arXiv, 1712.05526 (2017).

[10] C.-H. CHENG, C.-H. HUANG, AND H. YASUOKA, *Quantitative projection coverage for testing ml-enabled autonomous systems*, arXiv, 1805.04333 (2018).

[11] J. J. CHILENSKI AND S. P. MILLER, *Applicability of modified condition/decision coverage to software testing*, Software Engineering Journal, 9 (1994), pp. 193–200.

[12] K. CZARNECKI AND R. SALAY, *Towards a framework to manage perceptual uncertainty for safe automated driving*, in International Conference on Computer Safety, Reliability, and Security, Springer, 2018, pp. 439–445.

[13] D. DHEERU AND E. KARRA TANISKIDOU, *UCI machine learning repository*, 2017.

[14] M. DOUTHWAITE AND T. KELLY, *Safety-critical software and safety-critical artificial intelligence: Integrating new practices and new safety concerns for AI systems*, in Evolution of System Safety, Proceedings of the Twenty-sixth Safety-Critical Systems Symposium, Safety-Critical Systems Club, 2018. ISBN 978-1979733618.

[15] EUROPEAN AVIATION SAFETY AGENCY, *Certification specifications for aeroplane flight simulation training devices*, tech. rep., European Aviation Safety Agency, 2012.

[16] J. M. FARIA, *Non-determinism and failure modes in machine learning*, in 2017 IEEE International Symposium on Software Reliability Engineering Workshops (ISSREW), IEEE, 2017, pp. 310–316.

[17] A. Ferrando, L. A. Dennis, D. Ancona, M. Fisher, and V. Mascardi, *Recognising assumption violations in autonomous systems verification*, in Proceedings of the 17th International Conference on Autonomous Agents and MultiAgent Systems, International Foundation for Autonomous Agents and Multiagent Systems, 2018, pp. 1933–1935.

[18] J. Garcia and F. Fernández, *A comprehensive survey on safe reinforcement learning*, Journal of Machine Learning Research, 16 (2015), pp. 1437–1480.

[19] J. Gilmer, L. Metz, F. Faghri, S. S. Schoenholz, M. Raghu, M. Wattenberg, and I. Goodfellow, *Adversarial spheres*, arXiv, 1801.02774v2 (2018).

[20] I. J. Goodfellow, J. Shlens, and C. Szegedy, *Explaining and harnessing adversarial examples*, in Proceedings of the 3rd International Conference on Learning Representations, 2015.

[21] T. Gu, B. Dolan-Gavitt, and S. Garg, *Badnets: Identifying vulnerabilities in the machine learning model supply chain*, arXiv, 1708.06733 (2017).

[22] R. Guidotti, A. Monreale, S. Ruggieri, F. Turini, F. Giannotti, and D. Pedreschi, *A survey of methods for explaining black box models*, ACM Computing Surveys (CSUR), 51 (2018), p. 93.

[23] G. Haixiang, L. Yijing, J. Shang, G. Mingyun, H. Yuanyue, and G. Bing, *Learning from class-imbalanced data: Review of methods and applications*, Expert Systems with Applications, 73 (2017), pp. 220–239.

[24] B. Hamner, *Machine learning gremlins.* Presented at the 2014 O'Reilly Strata Data Conference in Santa Clara, 2014.

[25] R. Hawkins, I. Habli, and T. Kelly, *The principles of software safety assurance*, 31st International System Safety Conference, Boston, Massachusetts USA, (2013).

[26] L. A. Hendricks, Z. Akata, M. Rohrbach, J. Donahue, B. Schiele, and T. Darrell, *Generating visual explanations*, in Proceedings of the 14th European Conference on Computer Vision, 2016, p. 3–19.

[27] HM Government, *The Key Principles of Cyber Security for Connected and Automated Vehicles*, HM Government, 2017.

[28] ISO, *Road vehicles - functional safety*, Tech. Rep. ISO 26262, ISO, 2011.

[29] C. Jones, R. Bloomfield, P. Froome, and P. Bishop, *Methods for Assessing the Safety Integrity of Safety-related Software of Uncertain Pedigree (SOUP).*, HSE Books, 2001.

[30] A. Krizhevsky, I. Sutskever, and G. E. Hinton, *Imagenet classification with deep convolutional neural networks*, in Advances in neural information processing systems, 2012, pp. 1097–1105.

[31] Z. C. Lipton, K. Azizzadenesheli, A. Kumar, L. Li, J. Gao, and L. Deng, *Combating reinforcement learning's sisyphean curse with intrinsic fear*, arXiv, 1611.01211 (2016).

[32] G. Mason, R. Calinescu, D. Kudenko, and A. Banks, *Assured Reinforcement Learning with Formally Verified Abstract Policies*, 2017.

[33] C. Menon and R. Alexander, *A safety-case approach to ethical considerations for autonomous vehicles*, in Proceedings of the 12 IET International Conference on System Safety and Cyber Security, IET, 2017.

[34] A. S. Morcos, D. G. T. Barrett, N. C. Rabinowitz, and M. Botvinick, *On the importance of single directions for generalization*, arXiv, 1803.06959 (2018).

[35] J. G. Moreno-Torres, T. Raeder, R. Alaiz-Rodríguez, N. V. Chawla, and F. Herrera, *A unifying view on dataset shift in classification*, Pattern Recognition, 45 (2012), p. 521–530.

[36] A. ODENA AND I. GOODFELLOW, *Tensorfuzz: Debugging neural networks with coverage-guided fuzzing*, arXiv, 1807.10875 (2018).

[37] K. POHL AND A. METZGER, *Software product line testing*, Communications of the ACM, 49 (2006), pp. 78–81.

[38] D. POWELL, J. ARLAT, Y. DESWARTE, AND K. KANOUN, *Tolerance of design faults*, in Dependable and Historic Computing, Springer, 2011, pp. 428–452.

[39] M. T. RIBEIRO, S. SINGH, AND C. GUESTRIN, *Why should i trust you?: Explaining the predictions of any classifier*, in Proceedings of the 22nd ACM SIGKDD International Conference on Knowledge Discovery and Data Mining, ACM, 2016, pp. 1135–1144.

[40] RTCA, *Design assurance guidance for airborne electronic hardware*, Tech. Rep. DO-254, RTCA, April 2000.

[41] ——, *Software considerations in airborne systems and equipment certification*, Tech. Rep. DO-178C, RTCA, December 2011.

[42] ——, *Software tool qualification considerations*, Tech. Rep. DO-331, RTCA, December 2011.

[43] R. SALAY AND K. CZARNECKI, *Using machine learning safely in automotive software: An assessment and adaption of software process requirements in iso 26262*, arXiv, 1808.01614 (2018).

[44] R. G. SARGENT, *Verification and validation of simulation models*, in Simulation Conference (WSC), Proceedings of the 2009 Winter, IEEE, 2009, pp. 162–176.

[45] C. SCHORN, A. GUNTORO, AND G. ASCHEID, *Efficient on-line error detection and mitigation for deep neural network accelerators*, in International Conference on Computer Safety, Reliability, and Security, Springer, 2018, pp. 205–219.

[46] S. SRISAKAOKUL, Z. WU, A. ASTORGA, O. ALEBIOSU, AND T. XIE, *Multiple-implementation testing of supervised learning software*, in Proc. AAAI-18 Workshop on Engineering Dependable and Secure Machine Learning Systems (EDSMLS), 2018.

[47] N. SRIVASTAVA, G. HINTON, A. KRIZHEVSKY, I. SUTSKEVER, AND R. SALAKHUTDINOV, *Dropout: a simple way to prevent neural networks from overfitting*, The Journal of Machine Learning Research, 15 (2014), pp. 1929–1958.

[48] Y. SUN, M. WU, W. RUAN, X. HUANG, M. KWIATKOWSKA, AND D. KROENING, *Concolic testing for deep neural networks*, arXiv, 1805.00089 (2018).

[49] C. SZEGEDY, W. ZAREMBA, I. SUTSKEVER, J. BRUNA, D. ERHAN, I. GOODFELLOW, AND R. FERGUS, *Intriguing properties of neural networks*, arXiv, 1312.6199 (2013).

[50] J. W. TUKEY, *Exploratory data analysis*, vol. 2, Reading, Mass., 1977.

[51] S. WACHTER, B. MITTELSTADT, AND C. RUSSELL, *Counterfactual explanations without opening the black box: Automated decisions and the gdpr*, arXiv, 1711.00399 (2017).

[52] K. WAGSTAFF, *Machine learning that matters*, in Proceedings of the 29th International Conference on Machine Learning, 2012, 2012, pp. 529–536.

[53] G. M. WEISS, *Mining with rarity: A unifying framework*, ACM Sigkdd Explorations Newsletter, 6 (2004), pp. 7–19.

[54] Y. YANG, M. HE, M. LI, Q. WANG, AND B. BOEHM, *Phase distribution of software development effort*, in Proceedings of the Second ACM-IEEE International Symposium on Empirical Software Engineering and Measurement, ESEM '08, New York, NY, USA, 2008, ACM, pp. 61–69.

[55] Y. ZHANG, Y. CHEN, S.-C. CHEUNG, Y. XIONG, AND L. ZHANG, *An empirical study on tensorflow program bugs*, in Proceedings of the 27th ACM SIGSOFT International Symposium on Software Testing and Analysis, ISSTA 2018, New York, NY, USA, 2018, ACM, pp. 129–140.

# Appendix F   Contributors

This document has had the benefit of contributions from a large number of people, who work for a variety of organisations, which collectively span a range of different sectors. Note that contributions have been made on an individual basis and, in particular, the inclusion of an individual or organisation in the following list does *not* necessarily mean that individual or organisation agrees with the entire contents of the document.

Contributors include:

- Rob Alexander, University of York

- Rob Ashmore, Dstl

- Andrew Banks, LDRA

- John Birch, Horiba-MIRA

- Ben Bradshaw, ZF

- John Bragg, MBDA UK Ltd.

- Lavinia Burski, AECOM

- John Clegg, Independent (ex-QinetiQ)

- Timothy Coley, XPI Simulation

- Chris Harper, Atkins

- Neil Lewis, Dyson

- Catherine Menon, University of Hertfordshire

- Ken Neal, Ebeni

- Ashley Price, Raytheon

- Stuart Reid, STA Consulting

- Roger Rivett, Jaguar Land Rover

- Philippa Ryan, Adelard LLP

- Alan Simpson, Ebeni

- Rod Steel, Thales

- Nick Tudor, D-RisQ

- Stuart Tushingham, Altran

This page is intentionally blank

Printed in Great Britain
by Amazon